Cello Time Sprinters

Cello accompaniment book

Kathy and David Blackwell

Teacher's note
These duet parts are written to accompany the tunes in *Cello Time Sprinters*. They are an alternative to the piano accompaniments or CD, and are not designed to be used with those items.

We are grateful to Alison Ingram and Claire Saddler for all their help in road-testing these duets.

Kathy and David Blackwell

MUSIC DEPARTMENT

OXFORD
UNIVERSITY PRESS

OXFORD
UNIVERSITY PRESS

Great Clarendon Street, Oxford OX2 6DP,
United Kingdom

Oxford University Press is a department of the University of Oxford.
It furthers the University's objective of excellence in research, scholarship,
and education by publishing worldwide. Oxford is a registered trade mark of
Oxford University Press in the UK and in certain other countries

This collection © Oxford University Press 2005 and 2014

Unless marked otherwise, all pieces are by Kathy and David Blackwell and are
© Oxford University Press. All traditional and composed pieces are
arranged by Kathy and David Blackwell and are © Oxford University Press.
Unauthorized arrangement or photocopying of this copyright material is ILLEGAL.

Kathy and David Blackwell have asserted their right under the Copyright,
Designs and Patents Act, 1988, to be identified as the Composers of this Work.

Database right Oxford University Press (maker)

Impression: 9

All rights reserved. No part of this publication may be reproduced,
stored in a retrieval system, or transmitted, in any form or by any means,
without the prior permission in writing of Oxford University Press

Permission to perform the works in this anthology in public
(except in the course of divine worship) should normally be obtained from
a local performing right licensing organization, unless the owner or the occupier
of the premises being used already holds a licence from such an organization.
Likewise, permission to make and exploit a recording of these works
should be obtained from a local mechanical copyright licensing organization

Enquiries concerning reproduction outside the scope of the above
should be directed to the Music Rights Department, Oxford University Press, at
music.permissions.uk@oup.com or at the address above

ISBN 978-0-19-340116-7

Cover illustration by Martin Remphry

Music and text origination by Julia Bovee
Printed in Great Britain on acid-free paper by
Halstan & Co. Ltd, Amersham, Bucks.

Contents

1. Carnival jig 5
2. Spic and span 6
3. Out of the question 7
4. Stop—start 8
5. River song 9
6. Overture: A Baroque celebration 10
7. Going fourth 11
8. City streets 12
9. Minuet (Mozart) 13
10. Metro line 14
11. Falling leaves 15
12. Holiday in Havana 16
13. Swing low, sweet chariot 18
14. Night shift 17
15. Le Tambourin (Rameau) 19
16. Scarborough Fair 20
17. Beyond the horizon 21
18. Sto me 22
19. Bourrée (Stölzel) 22
20. Andante (Elgar) 24
21. Joker in the pack 25
22. Sarabande (Handel) 26
23. Comin' home 28
24. Sprint finish 30
25. In memory 31
26. Some day 32
27. Wild West 34
28. Je pense à toi 36
29. Russian wedding 38
30. Two songs from Dichterliebe (Schumann) 40
31. Latin nights 42
32. 4th dimension 46
33. Fifth Avenue 44
34. Seventh heaven 47
35. Jubilate Deo (Mozart) 48
36. Banuwa 48

1. Carnival jig

2. Spic and span

KB & DB

Variation: try playing with 2 semiquavers to each note:

3. Out of the question

Play questions and answers in this duet, returning to the chorus after each verse.
Make up and write down a question and answer of your own in the 3rd verse. Add your own dynamics!

4. Stop—start

5. River song

Flowing
KB & DB
p dolce e espress.
p dolce e espress.
5
9
mf
mf
13
mp
17
rall.
p
mp
p

6. Overture

A Baroque celebration

7. Going fourth

KB & DB

8. City streets

9. Minuet

10. Metro line

11. Falling leaves

12. Holiday in Havana

13. Swing low, sweet chariot: next page

14. Night shift

KB & DB

13. Swing low, sweet chariot

Play the second chorus as a canon, with the second part entering after a minim at *.
Count carefully in bar 20! Also try as a canon in 3 or 4 parts.

15. Le Tambourin

J. Ph. Rameau (1683–1764)
(adapted)

16. Scarborough Fair

17. Beyond the horizon

18. Sto me

Bulgarian trad.

19. Bourrée

G. H. Stölzel (1690–1749)

Adapted from the Clavierbüchlein for Wilhelm Friedemann Bach.

20. Andante

Edward Elgar (1857–1934)

21. Joker in the pack

22. Sarabande

G. F. Handel (1685–1759)
(adapted)

17
mp
mp
21
cresc.
mf
1
cresc.
mf
25
2
f
f
poco rit.
29
4
1
4

23. Comin' home

24
pizz.
mf
(arco)
(mf)
30
arco
(mf)
2
2
36
cresc.
f
ff
cresc.
f
ff
41
dim.
mf
rall.
pizz.
dim.
mf
pizz.

24. Sprint finish

25. In memory

(for Eileen)

26. Some day

KB & DB

21
mf
mf
26
31
cresc.
cresc.
37
1
mp
mp
42
1
Slower
p
p

27. Wild West

16
cresc.
cresc.
f
f
20
24
28
ff
ff

28. Je pense à toi

(for Clare)

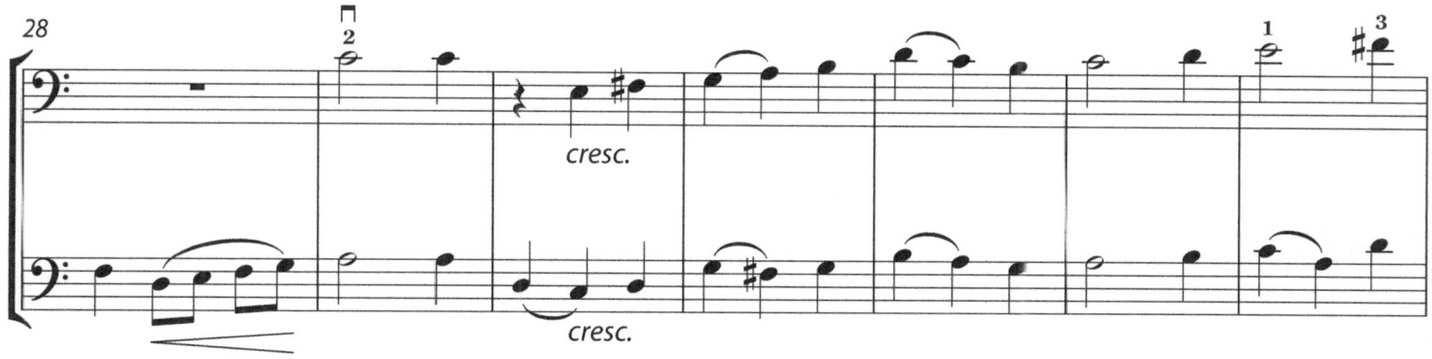
28
cresc.
cresc.

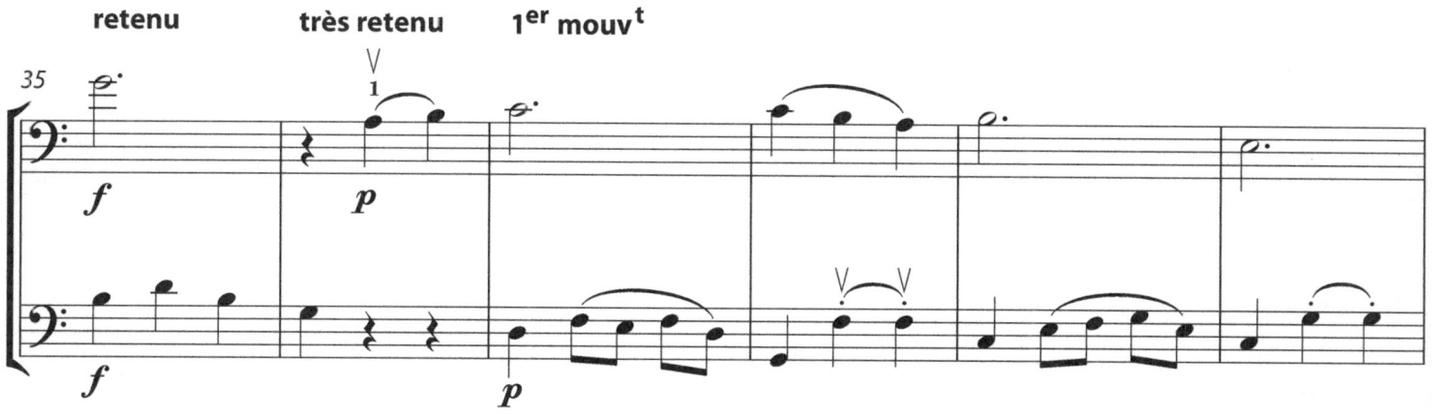
retenu
très retenu
1er mouvt
35
f
p
f
p

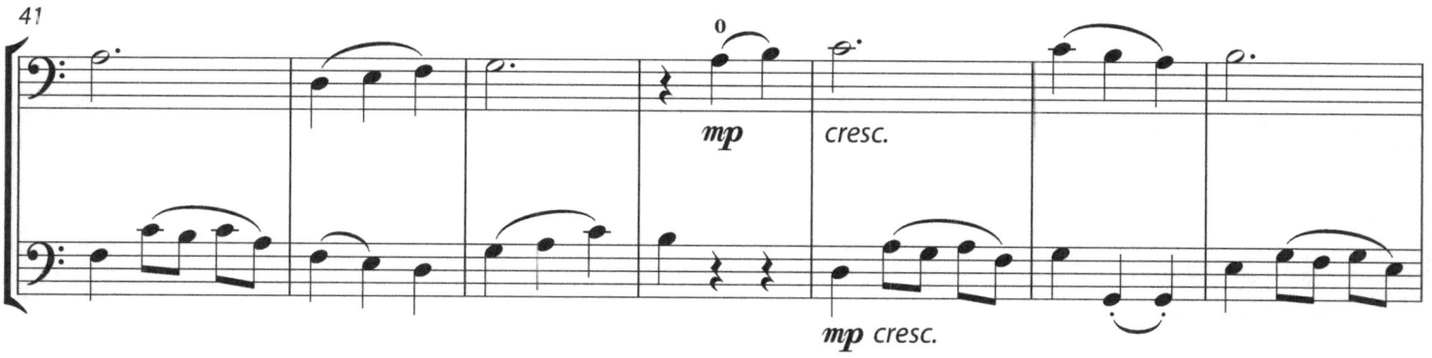
41
mp
cresc.
mp cresc.

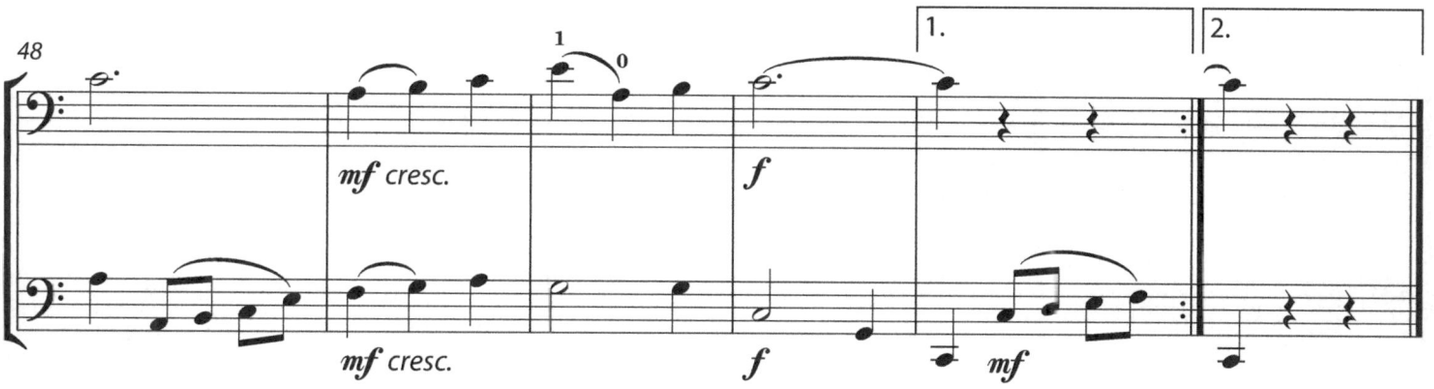
48
1.
2.
mf cresc.
f
mf cresc.
f
mf

29. Russian wedding

27
f
arco
f
p
pizz.
p
34
Slower
mf
arco
mf
a tempo
41
mp
mp
48
f
f
cresc.
cresc.
54
ff
ff

30. Two Songs from Dichterliebe

Robert Schumann (1810–56)
(adapted)

1. The lovely month of May

The repeat is written out in the cello part.

2. The rose and the lily

31. Latin nights

Tango

2.
Slow
18b
f
p
f
p
accel. poco a poco
cresc.
1
cresc.
a tempo
22
2
mf
3
mf
4
f
più mosso
25
4
f
f
f
29
1
2
3
32
4
ff
ff

32. 4th dimension: page 46

33. Fifth Avenue

(for lain)

Nos. 32 and 33 are reversed to avoid a page turn.

19
24
(1)
mp
cresc.
mp
cresc.
28
3
0
f
f
1.
mp
mp
32a
2.
f
ff
ff

32. 4th dimension

34. Seventh heaven

Dominant seventh study

Tap your cello with your left hand.

35. Jubilate Deo

Play this round in 2 or more parts, entering at *:

W. A. Mozart (1756–91)

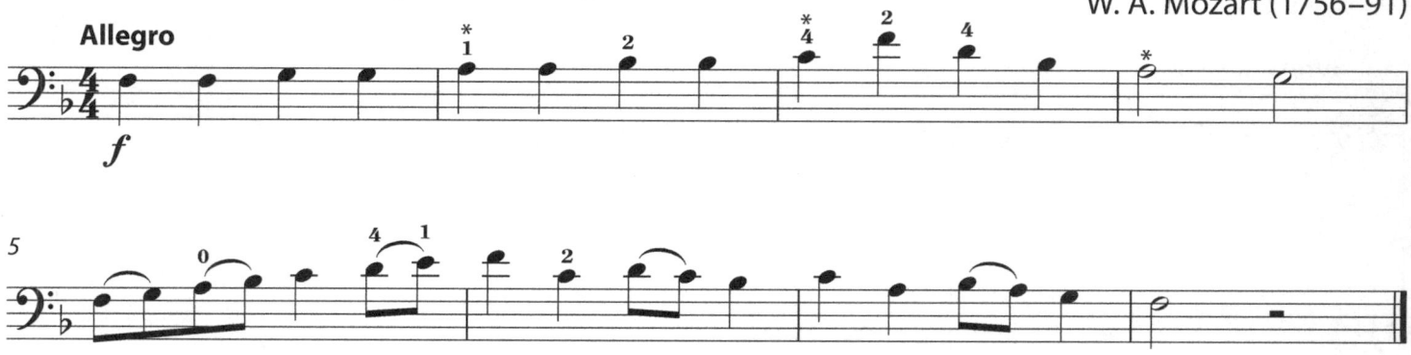

36. Banuwa

Play this round in 2 or more parts, entering at *:

African